Anna Gannon

The Song of Stradella

Anna Gannon

The Song of Stradella

ISBN/EAN: 9783337850791

Printed in Europe, USA, Canada, Australia, Japan

Cover: Foto ©Thomas Meinert / pixelio.de

More available books at **www.hansebooks.com**

THE SONG OF

𝕾𝖙𝖗𝖆𝖉𝖊𝖑𝖑𝖆

AND OTHER SONGS

Written by ANNA GANNON

PHILADELPHIA AND LONDON
J. B. LIPPINCOTT COMPANY
1899

TO THE

DEAR AND HONORED MEMORY

OF

THOMAS GANNON

CONTENTS

Contents

A DREAM OF SHAKESPEARE'S WOMEN

[As read by Miss Julia Marlowe]

In fair Virginia's heart there is a wood
  Where still the deer in careless freedom roams;
All night the owl, from 'neath his friar hood,
  Daunts with grim stare, the ever-wanton
    gnomes.
A sombre scene by night, but when bright dawn
  With mellow sunshine fills this garden spot,
When sweet birds sing, and leaps the gentle
    fawn,
  It seems, on earth, a fairer place is not.
'Twas here a child of song had chanced to stray;
  All night he'd wooed his worshipped Muse in
    vain,
And now the beauty that around him lay
  Gladdened his heart and soothed his tired
    brain.
"Oh, not in Arden was a lovelier wood,"
  He said, "And it would truly perfect be,
If but Orlando's fair one only could
  Come forth and give me her sweet company!"
His tired head upon the moss was laid,
  But ere his flagging senses sunk to rest

A Dream of Shakespeare's Women

He started. At his side a sweet voice said,
    " What though my woman's form like man be
        dressed ;
Beneath this rough attire there is a heart
    That would be brave—that would not weak-
        ness know,
But, like these garments, play a manly part—
    I would that I a bolder front could show."
'Tis Rosalind, " in youth's sweet prime," that
        stands
    Beneath a tree on which is carved her name,
And as she reads, she thinks of him whose hands
    Have cut the oak, his constant thought to
        frame.
A breath of the " sweet South" now filled the
        wood
    And all the grass took on a golden green,
As o'er it came, of visions the most fair,
    Young Juliet. Not all the jewelled sheen
That clasped her robes or bound her dusky hair
    Could dim the brightness of her eyes, that yet
Excelled them. From their depths the soul so
    rare
    Shone the more brightly, that 'twas richly set.
And when she spoke, she told a tale divine,
    Of moonlight nights beneath Italian skies
When she, the last of Capulet's great line,
    Had answered Romeo's impassioned sighs.

A Dream of Shakespeare's Women

And when the music of her rich low voice
   Had ceased, behold! appeared a laughing face,
A face to make your very heart rejoice,
   Had not a mocking smile half-marred its grace.
'Tis Beatrice, " in fancy free," who rails
   At all that is most dear to woman's heart,
Whose wit, " all mirth, no matter," never fails
   To give to satire's edge some playful part.
But hark! this sad sweet strain that fills the
     wood,
   Is it an earthly presence comes this way?
Ophelia! thou wert far too soft—too good!
   Oh, graceful child of Nature! Rose of May!
Yet rose that faded in the morning light,
   Thou singst thine own sad requiem, in truth,
Since o'er thy mind there fell the cruel blight
   That brought thee death in life and age in
     youth.
A spirit, yet on earth, she passed along—
   The glad birds ceased their tuneful notes—to
     brood.
The sunshine wavered and the brooklet's song
   Was hushed a moment in the silent wood.

But now the birds are challenged from their rest,
   The sound of silv'ry flute and harp floats by—
The air holds fragrant odors of the East,
   All-glorious Cleopatra draweth nigh;

A Dream of Shakespeare's Women

And as she spoke, long ages rolled away,
  The forest dimmed, then faded from her sight;
She lived again on fateful Actium-day,
  And heard death-cries from off her rocky
    height.
Once more she stood within the camp to try
  Her old allurements on her Roman slave—
" And yet, again, I see thee, Antony,
  Leave honor—all—and follow me, my brave !"
So speaks the " rare Egyptian," in whose smile
  There is a nation's fall.   Ah, cruel queen !
'Twas well to call thee " serpent of old Nile,"
  For, serpent-like, into the hearts of men
Thou glidest, and thy all destroying path
  Left poison in its trail.   Yet not content
With heart alone.   Thy fascination hath
  A power to seize the soul.   Oh ! wast thou sent
To bring fair Egypt to the lowly dust;
  To give to tyrant hands those fields of gold,
The glory of long centuries—all lost—
  With conquered nations is thy story told.
The dread enchantress gone, the tainted air
  Resounds with cries of mingled rage and hate,
And witches with wild eyes and matted hair
  Possess the wood, and chanting mock at Fate.
And closely in their train comes one accursed,
  Who shrinks in horror from her own white
    hand,

A Dream of Shakespeare's Women

Whose eyes see but one sight—a crime, the worst
    That e'er Ambition knew or Treach'ry
        planned.
Yet not Orestes in the Furies' power
    And not Prometheus on his high rock chained
Knew all the torments that each dragging hour
    Brought to this life while wretched life re-
        mained.
But now, as oft, when ignorance supreme
    Too long has held its unabated sway,
Upon the dark there comes a light whose gleam
    Shall pierce the clouds and scatter night away.
Thus in the troubled wood shone Portia's face,
    And thus shall Learning's ray still conquer
        night;
For, as the "mind glowed 'neath each lovely
        grace,"
    So shall expand all good in reason's light.
And thus the poet mused, while Portia stood,
    In cap and gown, as though for justice still
She would have asked. Here, in the silent wood,
    She might have spoken, but a voice, so shrill,
So loud, broke out that e'en the "murm'ring
        brook"
    For very shame was quiet. On near view
The owner of that voice had not the look
    A shrew should have, for this was Kate, "the
        shrew,

A Dream of Shakespeare's Women

And Kate, the curst," that evermore did scold;
   Till, as she nearer came, the poet tried
To find a refuge elsewhere, for, though bold,
   He now felt timid, but the maiden spied
His effort at escape, and nearer strode,
   When, starting up, the poet looked about
And nothing saw but the same lovely wood
   That in its smiling beauty seemed to flout
Dreamers and dreams. But still he heard the
     sound,
   And, looking up, beheld a chatt'ring jay
In the green boughs above. All else around
   Was silent. Over all the sunlight lay,
And where the crystal waters caught the gleam
   They shone like rarest gems. In such a
     place,
What wonder that the poet's vivid dream
   Seemed touched with something of the
     Master's grace !
" And did I only dream," perplexed, he thought,
   " And heard I not sweet Rosalind's complaint ?
Or Juliet's confession ? Was there naught
   But silence here ? Alone—did Mem'ry paint
The forms that lately seemed to move and speak ?
   Yet shall they live till Time has passed away ;
And while from Time an added charm they
     take,
   Yet shall they keep their magic of to-day.

A Dream of Shakespeare's Women

Oh, thou who knew so well the human heart,
   Great Shakespeare! It was thine to touch the
      chord
That makes the world akin! Yet not of Art
   So much as Nature hadst thou. At thy word
Came Virtues, Graces, Loves, with flying feet."
   But now the length'ning shadows on the grass
Aroused the poet from his rev'rie sweet;
   And thus, reluctantly, he left the place
That in the closing twilight seemed so fair,
   As though of tired earth it had no part,
As though the breath of Eden lingered where
   The woodland sleeps in fair Virginia's heart.

STRADELLA

'Twas long ago, and far away in Rome,
   There, 'neath her hills, a cow'ring hamlet
      lay:
Still in the shadow of St. Peter's dome,
   Yet from her message ever far away.
For dark the lives of those that dwelt therein;
   Nor faith nor virtue in that hamlet thrived,
And unto them are writ black deeds of sin.
   'Twas here the very prince of ruffians lived
That were of Italy the scourge and shame.
   Long feared as bandit of the clouded hills,

Stradella

Romarcus bore a deeper, lurid fame
  As cold assassin! His the name that thrills
The peasant heart with horror, and the cheek
  Of Roman manhood still has paler grown
If, on belated journey, should awake
  Some passing thought of him. For ne'er was
    known
The time, nor place, nor piteous circumstance
  That stayed Romarcus. In his den, alone,
He sat one night, all idly watching dance
  High shadows from his flick'ring fire. None
Might guess the thoughts of that half-savage
    brain,
  Nor whither travelled back his memory.
Light on the thatched roof fell the springtide
    rain—
  And springtide hath her witchcraft. Well
    't may be
The reason why, when lulled by gentle sound
  Of raindrops, as Romarcus dozed in sleep
He writhed once in agony profound.
  He woke, and felt as he had drunken deep
Of bitter, bitter potion. What the thought,
  That, all alone, unseen of ribald band,
Had thus a coward of Romarcus wrought?
  Yet not with curses woke he, tho' his hand
Cuffed the great hound that hastened to his knee,
  But sudden strode to where a flagon stood

Stradella

And quaffed the burning brandy long and free.
    Then, as before, he heard thro' the deep wood
The sounds of storm, and then, as not before,
    Some alien sounds without.   Upon his feet
With ears alert and eyes alight, no more
    He sleeps—but roused to life of fever-heat,
He listens—in his face a demon light.
    "It is a horse's hoof upon the ground!"
He muses: "Well, a halting-place you've found,
    Don Traveller, where you may halt for aye,
Nor e'er take up your journey."   To the end
    Of the steep pathway draws the rider nigh.
Over the chief's swift "Halt!" he laughs, "Ho,
    friend!"
    "Prove it," the stern voice answers. "I am
    one,"
The rider speaks, "who hath an enemy,
    And none can be my friend but thou alone.
I have brought gold, and freely give it thee."
    Darkly divining what the stranger bore
Within his heart, Romarcus threw aside
    All weapons and flung open wide the door.
There on the threshold stood, with mien of pride,
    A handsome stranger dressed in richest cloth,
A man of rank, who straightway handed out
    A bag of gold. Romarcus, nothing loath,
Accepting in grim silence. In some doubt,
    The stranger paused a moment, then began:

Stradella

" You shall have double when the deed is done."
 Romarcus answering : " Who is the man ?"
" The man 's Stradella, as a singer known ;
 His tall form ever in rich black is dressed,
His step is quick and light, his head held high,
 And many medals wears he on his breast———"
" Enough," broke in Romarcus ; " Where shall I
 Await him—when and where ?" The other
  spoke,
" To-morrow, Sunday, at the sunset hour.
 Be near St. Peter's doors at that last stroke
That tolls the vesper o'er. You might e'en
  cower,
 Dressed as a beggar, at Cathedral gate,
And gain a fuller view of all who come
 Without. Stradella will perhaps be late
To leave the church, and as he turns toward
  home
 Shadow him close, and when in darkened place
And well away from crowds—*you* have the rest !"
 An ugly smile gleaned in Romarcus' face.
" You have the situation well in hand ;
 Your plans lack naught but valor, do they,
  sir ?"
The wily stranger answered, calm and bland,
 " Your hand, Romarcus, never known to err,
Defying all detection, shall save mine
 The trouble ; but Stradella, knowing me

18

Stradella

And all who know my—hatred—would opine
  My business in his mere vicinity,
If evil followed. But no coward I,
  And I am desperate, Romarcus, too,
And long enough have I stood idly by
  And seen this man—still, what is this to you?"
For, as he spoke, Romarcus' gaze had strayed
  Unto the stranger's belt, and lingered where
A bright stiletto flashed, its carving made
  In strange device, and wrought with jewels rare.
" 'Tis a fine piece of steel," Romarcus said.
  " I have a better that I carry here,"
The man replied, " but this, 'tis said, was made
  For a De Medici—you may see where
Their crest, a crown, hath not had time to fade,
  And here, our own, a hawk with wings out-
      spread."
A while Romarcus with the bauble played.
  The stranger saw him restless, and quick said,
" Keep you the dagger as a gift, my friend,
  And tell me 'twill be done to-morrow eve."
Romarcus answered, " Yes, and let this end
  Our bargain."
           And the stranger took his leave.
Then long and deep and dark Romarcus thought,
  Holding the bright stiletto in the gleam
Of the swift dying fire, which yet caught
  And lit anew each flick'ring jewel's beam.

Stradella

" One stroke of this," he muttered; then to sleep
  He fell, a heavy stupor, not the rest
Of slumber.   All night long the storm raged deep,
  But ceased at morn.   Then all the world lay
      dress't
In smiles and sunbeams.   The old streets of Rome
  Took on a radiance, and the very air
Was sweet with April.   Where the great church
      dome
    Kissed the blue clouds, the sunlight glittered
      there
And glinted back, too dazzling to behold.
    And the half storm-drowned birds shot free
      their wings
And sang, " The springtime's on us!"   Young
      and old
    Reflected the calm joy glad weather brings.
As tender morning turned to fuller noon,
    And the soft air was warmed to richer life,
" It might be May-day, or the glad young
      June,"
    The people said, for all the land was rife
With whispers of the summer.   Soon it passed
    To afternoon, with cooler shadows.   Then
A still unearthly beauty seemed to rest
    Upon the city.   'Twas the hour when
The bell for prayer might any moment ring
    The vesper of St. Peter's, where the throng

Stradella

Ever increased to hear their idol sing—
  Stradella—loved, aye worshipped, of them
     long
And steadfastly.
            Stradella, ling'ring now
  By his wide opened windows, watched the
     day
Fade into twilight, still pondering how
  The human heart still hungers. Tho' his
     way
Thro' life might seem all starlit, yet
  Stradella sat alone, and, looking on
The fairness of this April, vague regret
  Came to him with a memory long gone.
Something akin to sorrow and to song
  Rushed on him thro' the beauty-laden hour,
Bringing lost Aprils, with their joys so long
  Departed; for, however life's full flower
Blooms in the present, yet the heart of man
  Turns to life's early blossoms, hailing them
The fairest of the bower. 'Twas so ran
  Stradella's thoughts. If it could be a dream—
These years of triumph—and he back again!
  Yea, all these golden honors lent of kings,
These medals—stars—they hang like so much
     pain
  Upon his breast. The sight of them but
     brings

Stradella

The thought of all the years that perished while
  He strove to earn them.
                   "Oh, thou days of truth,
Of early inspiration!   Hope's first smile!
  God, take Thou all, but bring my sweet, mad
      youth!"
Then on the air came the first vesper bell,
  And then, as ever, did Stradella's heart
Respond to that pure influence. "It is well,"
  He thought, "the present duty hath its part
To check the soul's vain longing." Then he
    passed
  Out thro' the street with light, quick step and
    head
Held high. Yet, whether 'twas the frail form
    dress'd
  In sombre black, or for his brow's pale shade,
Or for that very longing written there,
  Still, in Stradella there was that which drew
A loving pity e'en thro' homage. "Where
  So greatly dowered withal ('twas felt), there, too,
Must be a spirit greatly wrought and strung
  To painful tension ofttimes." When at last
Stradella reached the church and stood among
  The singers in the loft, he had not cast
E'en then the shadows from him.
                   There was one
  Who had well marked him as he entered there,

Stradella

Whose gaze that face and form had dwelt upon
   For one swift moment, then seemed lost in
      prayer.
It was a beggar, with his forehead bound
   In rags that half concealed his withered face.
He bent with years, and near him on the ground
   Long staff and bundle.   Still, he bore no trace
Of aught than some poor pilgrim at a shrine.
   Silent the church till now, when comes the train
Of acolytes, then myriad lights that shine
   In softened splendor, and the first faint strain
From the deep organ.   When, as with one soul,
   That vast assembly rose or knelt or prayed,
Still did the cow'ring beggar view the whole
   With cold indifference, tho' he essayed
Compliance with each custom.   Once, in truth,
   When first within the church, flashed on his
      brain,
With sound of those old chants, some tho't of
      youth :
   A village church and childhood's days again.
But swift he banished the strange thought and
      scorned
   The feeling it engendered.   Soon the air
Was full of odors from the incense burned
   And, silently, all heads were bowed in prayer.
Then through the misty aisles a sweet sound stole,
   Of dim and distant music.   Like a stream

Stradella

That falls in mountain ways, whose waters roll
   In rippling quietude, some faint notes came
From far above.   And, trembling on its chords,
   A deeper tone vibrated, then it ceased,
To rise again with sad impassioned words
   And sink again to stillness.   Then it passed
To higher rapture, for the lowlier prayer
   That pleaded Christ's compassion now grew
      strong,
And higher, holier, grander thro' the air
   Floated the angel voice.
                " Tho' ages long,
Thou One Almighty hath our sorrows known,
   Thou wilt have mercy!   Christ and man,
      forbear!
Ah, pity, yet!"
             But, now, into the tone
   Glided strange elements of vague despair,
A suddenness of terror that awoke
   Within the souls below an echoing fear,
All save one beggar, who with dark, fierce look
   Turned with contempt upon a wretch that
      near
Him stood, who held too long his labored
   breath
   And sighed aloud.
            Again the voice:
                " Lord, hear!

Stradella

Thou wilt not leave me to eternal death !"
    " Death !" 'Twas the beggar's turn to falter.
        Where
His hand had to his breast oft turned to clutch
    An object hidden there, that hand fell numb,
Nor could he yet regain the will to touch
    The thing again—and even thought seemed
        dumb
While still that voice, that voice that ever rose,
    In accents half divine, to Christ alone.
Yet not alone the singer, but all those
    Who heard the song adored their God, and
        none
So strange His works, that of the list'ning
        throng
    There is a beggar all unmanned—aye more,
Undemoned! Yet he would not from his ears
    Shut out that melody. But once before
To-day, and that in last night's troubled sleep,
    Has the strange influence of some far past
Come o'er him. He remembers now how deep
    His spirit writhed last night, when sleep had
        cast
On him, in dreams, unwonted thought of days
    Of his far childhood—and a village green
And young companions—of the gentler ways
    Of home. And how his waking tho't had
        been

Stradella

To curse such thoughts and drown them deep
    in drink.
    And now, to-day, the old chants brought back
        first
Unwished for thoughts.   But still, he need not
    think,
    And would not, till that cry, impassioned, burst
The armor of his dark, crime-laden soul.
    That, broken once, could not resist again
The entrance of that plea for pity.   All
    Stradella's life seemed hanging on that strain
That called to Christ's sweet mercy.
                      Dare the hand
    Still strike him?
                And Romarcus, in his heart,
Hath wavered once, and then, with swift com-
    mand
    Of those unhallowed laws that formed a part
Of his dark code of honor as a chief
    Of all assassins, to whom stalwart crime
Alone is " honor," still his old belief
    He strengthened in himself with:
                    " Not this time.
No, no, not this, some *other*, but not *him!*"
    Upon the morrow morn, as soft it rose—
The bright Italian morn—Stradella came
    Into the vine-crowned porch whose shadow
        throws

Stradella

Its shelter o'er his villa.   There he saw
  A bag of gold and, glittering thro' its knot,
A rich stiletto.   Still he stood, in awe
  At the strange sight, then, moving to the spot,
He took the blade, and looking on its rim
  Beheld the ancient crest—De Medici—
Another crest—of one who long had been
  His rival and his bitt'rest enemy!
Stradella felt the meaning of that gold
  And that stiletto left as warning there,
But whose the hand that saved him ne'er was told.
  But when the rival from his servants took
With falt'ring thanks the packet sealed, he
    clutched
It, nerveless, 'till he stood alone, then broke
  The cords.   There lay his bag of gold, un-
    touched,
And there gleamed his stiletto.   Nevermore
  In Rome was seen Stradella's enemy.
Creeping, disguised, that night he left the shore
  Forever.
          And Stradella?
                         Ah, well!   He
Flourished, the people's idol till the last.
  If ever came the dark thought unawares
Of this strange incident, all doubts he cast
  Aside and smiled, "I had some sweet one's
    prayers."

A LATE SUNRISE

SOMETIMES at close of day bursts forth the sun
In its full splendor, ev'ry cloud has flown
Before its swift surprisal; pale and long
The hours dragged without it. All of song
Has languished in its absence; now 'tis here
When the least dreamed of. And so may it fare
With a whole life of hope deferred; at last
Upon the soul's dull pathway may be cast
Some sweet revivifying warmth, as true
As the late sunbeam, that so softly threw
O'er a gray day its blessing, and the night
Of phantom fear may fade in new-found light.

TO THE HAWTHORN

COULD I recall but one day that has gone,
I would not ask to have the dearest one;
For deeply might to-morrow's shadows lie
Against the brightness of that time gone by.
But if I could bring back one vanished day,
Sweet Fancy! bring me one from glowing May,
And bonnie May in England! Might it be,

28

To the Hawthorn

That after endless leagues of changeless sea,
The dear earth smiles for us in new delight!
Thus it may be, for when on my charmed sight
Fell the fair picture of those hills and streams
And fields all radiant with the hawthorn gleams,
Then all my heart went Maying. Thro' the bloom
Of tangled blossoms with their pure perfume,
Re-lived for me the storied knights and maids
That passed through all these olden hills and glades.
Thro' woods like these went that frail flower-
　　like queen
Of saintly Arthur. These same skies have seen
Bright forms that unto ages past belong;
Here burning brows have turned their fire to
　　song—
Song born of this same beauty! What has been
Is now become a part of this still scene.
That, and the charm of springtime, ever young;
Such, that to think of it, my heart has sung
Its praises, while some fancy brings to-day
The early spring, the bonnie English May!

TIME'S TRACES

WE daily in the mirror gaze,
    Not seeing how
The hast'ning flight of wearing days
    Can touch the brow.

We seem, to-day, as yesterday.
    To-morrow, too, shall see
Us much the same.   Time creeps away
    So stealthily !

And then we meet a friend some day
    Of long ago ;
And wond'ring, in our hearts we say,
    " Have *I* changed too ?"

But just as swift his eyes have told
    The truth, alas !
Our friend has sorrowed to behold
    That time can pass.

FRANCE LA BELLE *

The hours on bright wings fly,
    France la Belle !
The southern nights drift by,
    France la Belle !
There rests upon thy brow
A glowing rose-wreath now,
    France la Belle !

A fair and flowery wreath !
    France la Belle !
Yet shines the steel beneath,
    France la Belle !
And down dream-haunted streets
The drum's wild pulse still beats,
    France la Belle !

SINCE LAST SWEET SPRING

Oh, dead year, dark year ! well that thou art past,
That left the heart, the hope so desolate !
Oh, slowly passing time, whose iron weight
Shall press upon the soul while life shall last !

---

* By permission of " The Quartier Latin."

31

Since Last Sweet Spring

Yet, strange indeed, O tyrant Grief, thou hast
A soft twin-sister, Sympathy, to wait
Awhile—then lead us from the dungeon gate
And loose the cords thou else would rivet fast.
Leading with light that nevermore shall fail,
Turns she the thought with her awak'ning breath
To a fair morn when Mary knelt in tears
Beside a vacant tomb till, starlike, pale
But radiant, spoke the angel—not of death,
But of New Life for all the endless years.

THE MAGNOLIA TREE

RICHLY purple and purely white
　　On the leafless trees they grow;
It is a strange and gladsome sight
　　To watch the flowers blow
Thro' a cold, bleak air o'er a frozen ground
While the breath of Eden floats around!

For theirs is a dream of the Orient,
　　Lemon and musk and myrrh.
Is it a far-off message sent
　　To this land of ours to stir
Our thoughts to the joys of another time,
A rich, new life in a heavenly clime?

"FROM WHENCE NO TRAVELLER RETURNS"

Up from the blackest night
  Ever comes morning:
After the winter-blight,
  Spring all-adorning!
Unto the leafless bough,
  Verdure, as ever—
All shall return.   And thou—
  Thou to me—never!

To the wood, silent long,
  Stilling its yearning,
Comes back an olden song;
  Blithe birds returning.
Now to the brooklets flow
  Music, as ever—
All shall return.   And thou—
  Thou to me—never!

33

THE FIRST THOUGHTS OF FAUST

Oh, happy heart!
I do not wish your life could join my own,
Sunbeam thou art,
Yet let me keep within the shade I've known.

Oh, heart of gold!
Longing and fear commingle till I know
Grief, new and old,
That shall be mine the while I stay or go!

Oh, loving heart!
You could not lift my burden with your joy;
Sorrow would start
In thy pure breast and all thy life destroy.

No, happy heart!
I shall not listen what the longing says;
When we two part,
Then joy and grief have gone their sep'rate
ways!

MARGUERITE AT THE SPINNING-WHEEL *

To Madame Calvé in "Faust"

Ah, Margherita, cease !
  I cannot look on thee
As now, girt round with peace,
  All spirit-pure and free,

Thou singest at the wheel.
  O passing moment, stay !
Let no new feeling steal
  One happy note away !

Uplifted song and heart,
  And eyes that seek the heaven—
O Nature, void of art !
  O Genius, sacred given !

Are these the wherewithal
  For aught but fairest ends ?
Shall e'en the wrapped bud fall ?
  Is't thus that Heaven lends

---

* By permission of " The Quartier Latin."

Marguerite at the Spinning-Wheel

Her graces as a snare?
　　Cease, Songbird! thy young faith
And ardor, pure and rare,
　　Foretell thy life, love, death!

ON PASSING THE IRISH COAST

Not through the ocean's waste had my heart
　　known
A moment's sadness or a sinking thought
Till thy dear hills arose, O strangely lone
　　Of nations!　How the very winds have caught
The sick cry of the ages!　Desolate!
　　It is the burden of thy seagulls' song!
The rocks re-echo till the dreary weight
　　Of sorrow falls, then, sobbing deep and long,
The waves rehearse thy ancient wrongs till I,
　　Who never knew thee, I could weep.　Oh,
　　　　where
Thy storied grandeur?　Where thy minstrelsy?
　　All lost?　But, no!　Did I not dream the air
Was full of mighty music?　'Twas a hand
　　Of wondrous force that smote those chords
　　　　of might,
And He that made shall yet attune this land
　　Of latent harmonies to love and light.

LONDON

At night I came to London town
And saw where, darkly shadowed down
Upon the Thames, Westminster lay.
Such dreams were mine!   I never may
Renounce their dim prophetic sway,
And yet my spirit felt the frown
        Of London town.

And when at last to rest laid down,
To peopled dreams in London town,
All thro' the night I felt the spell
Of old Westminster's mighty bell;
O'er heart and brain its message fell—
My spirit soared beyond the frown
        Of London town.

" Oh, not thro' rest came their renown,"
The spirit spoke, in London town;
" The loved, the great that England brings
To mingle with the dust of kings,
For, ever, Fame her laurel brings
To him who well would wear the crown
        In every town."

London

When I awoke in London town
And saw the sunlight shimmering down
Upon that wondrous Thames, I caught
Such hope divine as ne'er was wrought
From warning word, or sermon taught—
God's sunlight 'twas, despite the frown
      Of London town.

THE MEMORY OF MY OWN LAND

What tho' in other lands
    The days might lightly pass,
As silv'ry as the sands
    Within Time's olden glass?
When all fulfilled as Hope planned,
    The spirit stood apart—
The mem'ry of my own land
    Rose ever in my heart.

In joy, in love, in awe,
    Loomed up before my eyes
All dreaming Fancy saw
    Beneath the banished skies!
It was a passing pageant, and
    The soul still soared afar—
The mem'ry of my own land
    Hung o'er me like a star.

THE POET WYATT TO ANNE
BOLEYN

HEART of my heart, I remember
    All I have sworn to forget.
See! on Love's flames a last ember
    Gloweth and kindleth yet!
Only the night shall behold it;
    Starlight and song only know
How deep the heartstrings enfold it—
    Joy of my life—and its woe!

'Twas not that my idle dreaming
    Compassed the maiden most fair;
Nay! wert thou marred past all seeming,
    Still would thy love be my prayer!
Heart of my heart, I remember
    All I have sworn to forget.
See! on Love's flames a last ember
    Gloweth and kindleth yet!

WHILE a new sorrow holds, grief may be numb
   Or, of its own intensity, may die;
   We bid a parting spirit rest for aye,
Unknowing how in afterdays shall come
New pangs from that old wound. Yet there
     are some
   May sadly think of death " 'Tis well," but I,
   Hearing thy name still mingled with the cry
Of earth's unfortunates, cannot be dumb.

A beggar asks for alms in thy dear name;
   He once had asked in Christ's, but thou hadst
     been
   The gracious means wherewith a God had
     seen
Full many a sad prayer answered. This thy
     fame;
   " For deeds of love that now thou canst not
     screen,
Time! Let Love's incense all his memory
     frame!"

A SONG

You have heard the wild-bird singing
  When spring was newly born,
And with autumn's sadness ringing
  You have heard the wild-bird mourn ;
And your voice, your voice has yet
All the wild-bird's notes so sad, so sweet.
    Ah ! if I heard it again,
      Soft it would fall on my heart !
    Swift on its silvery strain
      Sorrowing care should depart.

Now that spring hath flown with gladness,
  And no longer wild-birds call,
'Tis the autumn's reign of sadness—
  On the heart its shadows fall ;
But your voice, your voice has yet
For all care a charm so sad, so sweet.
    Ah ! if I heard it again,
      Soft it would fall on my heart !
    Swift on its silvery strain
      Sorrowing care should depart.

WHEN THE HAWTHORN BLOOMS
AGAIN

No matter where the hearth is,
   The loving land of home,
When first the spring awakens
   My spirit swift would roam
Unto a land remembered—
   A dream all void of pain—
And I would be in England
   When the hawthorn blooms again.

For oh! once more to wander
   The mystic-scented glades,
Where old romance holds revel
   And legend haunts the shades!
Oh! never care should find me,
   And all my song's glad strain
Should be of " Bonny England
   When the hawthorn blooms again !"

DREAMS

Come back, sweet dreams!
So long you leave me that the Future seems
A poor, pale land, unbrightened by your gleams;
    Come, then, dear dreams!

Life has such care!
How shall it be if no illusion share
The burden with reality? Despair
    Creeps in with care.

But fancy's wings
The longed-for message from the far land brings!
Of heart's delight this bird of morning sings,
    Then mounts her wings.

Yet come, dear dreams!
I dare not be without you, since all seems
The shadowland unbrightened by your gleams;
    Come, then, sweet dreams!

THE SEASON OF SONG

Blame not the poets that they sing
   Forevermore of spring!
   A new world 'wakes
   When the old one breaks
Her last cold chain with mighty fling;
   Oh! to the dreamer's heart it seems
   That heaven nearer gleams!

While a sad season stayed, his cup
   With bitter dregs filled up.
   But now its gall
   Hath vanished—all!
A golden vintage he may sup,
   While but to live seems half divine—
   The very air is wine!

Then let them rave and let them sing
   Forevermore of spring!
   It is the time
   Of nature's rhyme;
Old pathways, silent long, shall ring,
   And song unsought for, too, shall start
   Within the singer's heart.

A VOICE

A voice that was beautiful spoke—
  Its words were so simple and true,
The "halt" by the wayside awoke
  And took up his journey anew.
The life that he deemed as well o'er,
  Now stirred in his bosom again ;
The sorrow that stung him before
  Seemed now but the shadow of pain.

A voice that was beautiful sang
  Of all that the heart longs to hear ;
The glad music, echoing, rang
  Long, late in the listener's ear,
Not dim or remote then, it seemed,
  The listener's longing desire ;
He hoped where he once had but dreamed,
  And wrought where he dared to aspire.

A SONG OF REST

I HEARD a song of rest so infinite
    That even thought was silenced, and a peace
Fell on the spirit softer than the light
    Of quiet stars when dreary day shall cease.

Who hath not drifted to that fairy shore?
    Who hath not longed to find that isle so blest,
Where hope shall cheat and fate betray no more,
    And all life's fever turn to dreamless rest?

TO THE MASK AND WIG CLUB

THE wiser heads of another day
Decided that work, all work and no play,
    Would make but a dull boy of Jack;
And the folks of to-day all merrily say
    They have found a fair way to bring back

To old heads the past, to young hearts the joys,
That the blithe hour brings with the merry-
        souled boys,
    Whether young or old, little or big;
And if mem'ry be sad, why, the present is glad
    When the toast is " The gay Mask and Wig!"

THE WEDDING-DAY

ONCE from a country inn I strayed,
And saw, slow-pacing 'neath her shade,
A woman old, yet in whose eye
Youth's light perhaps might never die.
For want of better else, I walked
Beneath her trees, and soon we talked;
The weather first, for old folks will
Of beldam nature chatter still;
The crops, the harvest, and the rest
Of country gossip, but no jest
Of mine could summon up a smile,
For she grew silent. In a while
She turned to me with motion swift,
That from her shoulders seemed to lift
Some years of age, and suddenly
She spoke with fervor, " Can it be
As bad as now it seems? I feel to-day
That some one drains my life away!
Yet well I know 'tis truth that's meant.
The truth! no vain presentiment!
Oft I have known what 'twas to be
Forewarned of ill that came to me,
But this—you might not call it grief,
And you may say 'tis past belief,

The Wedding-Day

A selfish heart should call it so—
Well, one's joy, aye, is other's woe.
To-morrow brings me grief—no joy—
'Twill see my hope, my life, my boy,
Unto another wend his way.
Alas! 'tis Robin's wedding-day!

" Yes! he and I were here alone,
The others one by one all gone.
His father, ah, so long ago,
And some are wedded, some laid low,
But with my Robin left, I knew
All grief might still be battled through.
Oh! thro' the worst, when most bereft,
I said, ' I have my Robin left.'
But now, but now, I see it all;
For me no more at even-fall
To wait his coming, nor to hear
The only voice that I hold dear.
He leaves me!   Old, alone, forlorn,
Yet must I strive to-morrow morn,
Strive to be happy, bright, and gay—
Alas! 'tis Robin's wedding-day!"

A VOYAGE

Can aught more peaceful be
Than May-Day on the sea?
The long still afternoons
Drift by like old love tunes.

Yes, 'tis a soft, sweet song—
The waves that splash along!
Yes, 'tis a siren sings,
And happy thoughts she brings.

Off where the water's blue
Hath merged the sky's fair hue;
We strive in vain to see
Where each hath ceased to be.

Thro' days that have not passed
A solitary mast,
How oft to those still skies
Our thoughts in prayer arise!

A MODERN SAINT

Was there a maiden like to you
When long ago an artist drew
A gentle Saint Cecilia? Naught
That his inspired brush has caught
But might have been from you derived.
Perhaps had you in his day lived,
And sat his model, we had seen
A rarer still, a statelier mien,
A brow more spiritually fair
Beneath the night-kissed parted hair!
Oh, Art unerring, quick to know,
Had made the old-time canvas glow,
While he, of insight swift and true,
Had given all time his dream of you.

"AUF WIEDERSEHEN"

The strains of Wiedersehen are sweet—
The glowing chords themselves repeat
        "We'll meet again!"
        Oh! happy then!

"Auf Wiedersehen"

Surpassing smooth it glides along,
As blithe as any wild-bird's song.
'Tis hope's attempt (delusion fair!)
To place again the perfume rare
Upon the sinking flower of spring,
For all in vain the echoes ring
    " We'll meet again !"
    For oh! till then!

A SONG OF RIZZIO TO MARY STUART

Forever lies a land beyond the sea, love ;
Say thou wilt wander there for aye with me, love ;
    Sorrow shall fly
    Beneath that sky,
And life a softly-passing dream shall be, love !

Oh ! like the rippling waves upon the sand, love,
Laughter and song shall rise in that fair land, love ;
    Oh ! wherefore wait
    In dreary state ?
My soul's true queen shall from all hearts com-
mand love !

JANE AUSTEN'S GARDEN

I⊤ is her garden, but she is not here—
Yet does the very air seem full of her!
The walls, so high, have never let too near
One alien breeze among her roses stir.
" Not what they were," they say, " when she
    was here,"
Yet here she found delight—her eyes have seen.
Often at dusk (for e'en loved work grows drear)
Has not this bower to her most welcome been?
She came with downcast eyes, and footsteps slow,
With the dream-people for still company ;
Here the true types of that far day would grow,
The young-yet Emma, or, one paler, she
Of patient love's duress, a pictured saint,
Anne Elliot (sweet Austen's self I know!)
And yet how many more of fiction quaint
Took life in this old garden!
                            Chill and low,
To-day, a summer storm hath bent the vines
And from the wall the blossoms pale float down
With their old-fashioned fragrance still entwines
Her memory with the spot that she hath known!

A SEAPORT TOWN

THE fogs of centuries have settled down
    Upon this time-worn town ;
Smoke, spray, and vapor, in a union drear,
    Have settled here.

The very sea in sullen stupor lies
    Reflecting duller skies ;
Steeples and roofs and buildings, sad and gray,
    Reeking with spray,

Seem to reproach the earth and sky, as they
    Most mournfully might say,
" None too great ever did the heavens bless,
    And man still less !"

CONTENT

THE days go on in measureless content,
  Peace holds the glass, and soothingly the
    sands
Move onward till the quiet hour is spent.
  Charge me not, Time ! That I with empty
    hands

Content

Sit in the ingle! I may start again
    With a new, quickened heart into the strife
Of the full field; know all the joy and pain
    That follows fast upon the active life.

But—ere the longing rise, or feeling's stress,
    Or the strong hope, to trust, perhaps, in vain,
Here, where fair peace seems smilingly to bless,
    Leave me a little while to dream again.

SONNET TO THE MARCH WINDS

Last night the March winds woke me and I went
    On their wild path with them thro' many a way
    That would escape me thro' the busy day.
With the wild winds that have their tremor sent
Over the graves, where I, alas, had meant
    To stand beside, to comfort and to pray:
    To make them glad—if mortal act so may!

They lie so lonely 'neath the chill moonlight!
    Had I been there to-day, as full I meant,
My prayer the softer to their slumber might
    Have sent them! Now the day fore'er is spent,
    And all the winds sob o'er my lost intent,
And all the winds sob out my lost " good-night!"

OF AN ELOQUENT PREACHER

In every word he saith,
Behold poor trampled Faith!
We hark to one who could
Aspire—if he would.

A master-mind, perplexed!
A spirit conscience vexed.
The dark, now pierced!   In vain—
He gropes in night again.

He speaks of souls long gone:
Le Blanc and Fénelon—
He points where in the past
The truth hath shone, at last!

Poor human minds distressed,
By all this doubt, possessed!
And what of those who caught,
Though late, the gleam they sought?

Oh thou, who would aright
Seek thou, that " Kindly Light!"
Find thou their courage bold!
Rest in His *poor, sad* fold!

ELLEN TERRY

Some say she is not human—
This strange elusive woman—
That she's some gay enchanting elf
    From out the sea or sky ;
        But I
Believe she's just her gracious self.

Some ever praise the acting,
And others, all-exacting,
Her silences adore. But when
    She speaks her own free mind,
        I find
She is the most attractive then.

Another generation
Shall list in veneration,
As all describe her haunting art,
    And sing her merits high.
        But I
Shall tell them of her gentle heart.

Fulham, England, August 26, 1898. '

THE SPRING SEA

EARTH has no words to say how fair
   The waves came in to-day !
The kingly sun upon them shone
   In a royal lover's way.
It seemed all music centred there,
   In the rippling water's play ;
The king above looked down in love
   Where the sparkling beauty lay !

ROMNEY'S WIFE

I WILL await you !   Others have to-day,
But I will have you sometime !   Bowed and gray

You may be—ah ! you will be, when you come,
Bowed with life's ev'ry storm, yet to your home—

The home my heart shall ever keep for you—
My straining vision brings you straight and true.

You loved me once—you do not hate me yet—
And I will not believe you can forget !

Romney's Wife

And I loved more in you than time can fade,
And hence I can await you.   You have said

We shall not meet again, but oh! we will,
And tho' my heart be heavy, sadder still

Shall yours be that day!   Others have to-day,
But I shall claim you sometime!   On your way

You will e'en miss me, for you cannot be
To any one quite what you were to me.

No word of mine shall call you back again,
But you will come without it.   In the pain

And heartache you so ill could bear alone,
Swift you will think of me, my longed-for one!

Then, tho' the years have never left a trace
Of aught that drew me in your loved, loved face,

I shall forgive the years that I have missed—
All the long years wherein we never kissed

Or spoke one word of loving.   When you come—
For ah! you will—with heart no more to roam.

Yes, others have to-day, but love can wait
That home-returning, sad and sick and late.

THE APRIL WAVES

If it only could last for ever!
  The springtide of the sea,
For I hold that its charm is never
  So deep and so grandly free.

In a moment the eyes, far ranging,
  Run sun-bright waters o'er ;
In the next, with April's changing,
  A lowering waste no more!

And again, in a mimic fury,
  A sodden sand they crash !
Then their April griefs they bury,
  And sink in a silken splash.

Then they slumber for hours together,
  And weary again of their rest,
Till we cannot (so charm they) tell whether
  Their calm or their storm is best.

A PORTRAIT *

BEAUTIFUL Sally Reams!
I look at your face till it seems
   The present is slipping away,
   And the dusk of a Southern day
Comes closing around me with all of its won-
    derful gleams.

I know but your pictured face—
Bright page, that no future shall trace—
   But I know, as a twice-told tale,
   That your charm could never fail,
That you seemed to be part of the South and
    its mystical grace.

Beautiful Sally Reams!
Was your heart what your image seems?
   Did you treasure the noble in youth,
   Tho' it came of the North or the South,
Long ago? Was there room for the North in
    the Southern girl's dreams?

---

* A portrait brought to the North after the Civil War.

THE EARLY LOST

[In memory of Francis Hazen.]

SHALL it be thus, the coming years
We hailed with hope—and face with fears?
Shall e'en the past be seen thro' tears
  For you, Fanny?

Was it that Eden-forms of light
Grew jealous of our poor earth-right,
And called their sister-spirit bright,
  "Return, Fanny?"

For thought of you is thought of song,
The light song of a heart so young
No years had aged, tho' brief or long
  Your life, Fanny.

Some bitterness the pen has weighed,
To think the Reaper had not stayed
In pity for so bright a maid—
  For you, Fanny!

THE HARP

THERE's a harp below in the street,
And its melody quaint and sweet
Hath brought back the song to-day
Of a harp that is far away.

And again the soft light shines
O'er a form that half reclines
By a golden harp whose chords
Have meaning too deep for words.

And meaning too deep for me,
Till I think that it should not be
That the sorrows we might forget
The vague, or the real regret,

Should be sung into life again
To the harp's vibrating pain !
They are past, and we would forget
Till the harp-strings whisper " Not yet !"

SONG TO THE LOST

"You will return," the night's first voice is
    sighing,
"Return, return!" the echoes long replying,
Twilight grows dense and shadows deeper falling
Upon a soul all sorrow-worn, are calling
          "Return! Return!"

Where e'er you are, does never mem'ry move
    you
To come again where once you loved to be?
Oh, dream you nothing of the hearts that love
    you,
Is there not even one your soul would see?

"Return, return!" the night's last voice is
    singing,
"Return, return!" the whisp'ring air is ringing
But once again! You cannot stay unheeding
All nature's voice and mine forever pleading
          "Return! Return!"

A PROMISE

Will I forget you? Never! Let the morn
   Forget to follow night—let everything
That's sweet and certain fail: yet must I mourn
   Your going while a hope divine shall sing
                  Of your return—again!

Can I forget you, ever? When each thought
   Of mine to you hath homage? If my days
Were crowned with riches, love and fame, all
     naught
   Would be their pow'r the spirit sad to raise,
                That looked for you—in vain!

I will forget you never! On your way
   May all that's bright attend you! Sorrowing
     cares
Shall pass you by, and o'er your ev'ry-day
   Unwonted joys shall smile, the while my
     prayers
             Must bring you back, again!

THE POET IN DESPAIR TO THE
MUSE

WHY do I wait for you?
Too long false hope hath led me, and I know
It is a doubtful pathway I would go—
A future fair confronts me, while I stay
To watch your light o' love shine o'er my way;
Till I could bid the very dawn of day,
    "Be late," for you!

I will not stay for you!
A thousand better hopes have left me while
I dreamed of many an hour you might beguile.
And now I have you not, and peace has flown
Will-o'-the-wisp! to lure the traveller on
Till his life's way grow dim and all unknown,
    Life's way, for you!

LOSS

[TRANSLATION]

THOU who wert near!
　How can it be
　That poor dim memory—
　Thou unto me—
Must evermore appear?

Strange will it be
　When thou art gone!
　And I, poor one! alone,
　Must live upon,
But what thou wert to me.

The coming years!
　Void though they be,
　Yet shall they pass for me!
　To-day's still misery
May fade in tears!

THE FOURTH OF JULY IN PARIS

WE hear them come!
With merry fife and drum,
And dancing, prancing hoof
   Of dashing horses' feet,
While many a bannered roof
   Resounds the stirring beat!

And love—not war,
Brings this gay band afar
'Neath summer sun to-day!
   But in fair brotherhood,
Our countrymen and they
   Who once beside them stood!

All honor be,
Oh generous France, to thee
Who late learned Freedom's truth,
   Yet lent thy gracious hand
To aid the towering youth
   Of our immortal land!

THE VALLEY OF THE SHADOW

" I shall go to him, but he shall not return to me."—
2 SAMUEL XII. 23.

IT is so quiet by the old church wall;
I wonder if you ever heed at all
That loved ones come, or what sad tears shall fall;

You could not lie so quiet if you knew
How many thoughts go onward still with you!
How 'tis but half a sorrow to be true!

I would not wake you from a sleep so blest:
I know you lie upon the just One's breast—
But—where *you* are, how sweet must be that
rest!

A rest from which I dare not wish you free;
I know you shall not rise and come to me,
That mine alone to you the path may be!

BASSANIO: WILLIAM TERRISS

WHERE's Bassanio, who taught us
   Friendship fair hath bonds of steel?
Where's the soldier-hero wrought us
   Loyalty or love to feel?

Into night hath all the lightness
   Faded? Nay, hope, trusting dreams
Some far clime hath new-found brightness
   Where the hero's brow still gleams.

GENERAL CUSTER

SAID one who knew the hero once,
   How oft I think of him!
Tho' later lights may flare, perchance,
   None can his glory dim!

He was a leader, first and last,
   For action framed and nerved;
(My calmer path in thought was cast,
   Yet each our Union served.)

69

General Custer

Full oft I watched him as I sat,
    (O'er work my head e'er bent)
Nor ceased with use to wonder at
    Each noble lineament!

His was a valor born within;
    A soul that fear defied!
His was a gallant cause to win,
    And a dashing horse to ride!

How I can see him—see him yet!
    Like a young God of War;
Astride a steed, all hotly wet,
    And mad with smoke and roar.

Full of the strife that filled the mind
    Of the rider brave and fair—
And still I see how on the wind
    Floated that flaxen hair—

Floated or fell to shoulder-length
    Neglected all, while he
Brought a brain's wealth and body-strength
    To ride to victory!

General Custer

Yet had he charms of peace, as well,
   And strength of sweetness, too,
And often on my ear there fell
   His laughter, ringing true.

And when he smiled, to me it seemed
   A living spark of light
Had flashed from eyes and lips, and gleamed,
   As though the latent Might—

The forces that we know not of
   In him were clearer than
We may oft see them rise and move
   In less God-gifted man.

Yes! like a meteor light he shone—
   And like the same he passed!
Into the darkness hath he gone—
   Glittering, to the last!

His was a valor born within;
   A soul that fear defied!
His was a gallant cause to win,
   And a dashing horse to ride!

OF MOURNING

Sometimes—I'd leave the whole of life to be,
Sweet one, with thee!
I have one wish—to sit with the forlorn,
Who (loved ones) mourn!

In their sad looks, for evermore I see
Some thought of thee;
I dream they held their loved and lost, Divine,
As I held mine!

So, could I take them to my heart, and say:
"With you I pray—
Gaunt sorrow stalks with you! at least, to-day,
The same our way;

Let me be with you, till your path is done,
You mourn some one!"
A little while with me the sad ones stay,
And then—away!

VILLA DES ACACIAS, IN THE BOIS
(PARIS)

"I have been here before."—DANTE ROSSETTI.

I KNOW this place so well!
  I have passed down this way—
The faint acacia-smell
        Of this café
Hath not come new to me, this summer day.

The blossoming boughs that twine,
  Beyond that counter where
Is ranged the red, red wine—
        All these were *there*,
And nothing new I see, in coming here!

'Twas thro' some path of sleep,
  Unto this spot I came
This wood—so green—so deep—
        It is the same!
Nothing to me is new—but its sweet name!

AFTER LOSS

I WENT within his room,
I thought to cast from out my soul the gloom
That overwhelmed the heart, and held the brain
In darkest thrall, and in that room again
      I stood as by his tomb.

      I watched sad autumn's rain
Come moodily against his window-pane
Thro' his loved trees I caught the storm's dull
      tone
And knew as surely as in grief's first moan
      That time had passed in vain.

      And vain poor hope's belief
That time shall blunt the edge of sharpest grief,
What tho' the fewer fall the mourner's tears,
This weight of loss that deepens with the years;
      No, call not this relief!

A LITTLE WHILE

A LITTLE while she lingered but to see
      What life could be
Within a charmèd circle that she drew,
      But passed not through.

As first she gazed, some triumph filled her eyes—
      A glad surprise—
Till something of the milder calm of thought
      Upon her wrought.

She was a looker-on ; she could but see
      What still must be,
And as she deeper saw, surprise again
      Turned into pain.

Swift change alone, she marked, seemed life's
    great law ;
      Her deep eyes saw
How sadly swift to one who giveth all
      Beyond recall.

THE ENCHANTED LAND

" It was the isle of ' It may not be,' "
    She said, " Where I lingered awhile,
And all that had ever seemed sweet to me
    I found on that charmed isle !

" Never loomed nature so dreamily fair,
    Never such sunlights set ;
Never such starlights rose as there
    In the land I cannot forget !

" Unto the isle of ' It may not be '
    I had gone with a heart aglow,
And hope and pleasure and song for me
    Seemed ever to rise and flow

" In sweet accord with the winds and waves
    That rose round that isle so free ;
There were joys I had dreamed the Eden saves
    In the isle of ' It may not be' !

" Too brief was my stay in a land so fair,
    Where joy thrilled in every breath,
For the waters changed as I sailed, and where
    The sea rose the shades seemed death.

The Enchanted Land

" The pale mists followed me from the shore,
  And the low waves moaned to me,
You are leaving your life for evermore
  In the land of ' It may not be' !"

THE TRUE

Tho' the fancy may stray
To the brilliant and gay,
However their glitter throw round us its strong
  dazzling hue,
Not for long they beguile ;
We but heed them awhile,
And our hearts shall come back to the good and
  the true !

Fair feature and form
The senses may storm ;
Enchantments like these shall delight us the
  while they are new,
But the lure shall not last—
And the glamour once past,
Our hearts shall come back to the good and the
  true.

ON A PORTRAIT OF LINCOLN

IF looks could speak, thy sad face would
  Tell all the noble life
  Of truth dethroning strife—
Of tyrant error slain, thou great and good!

Thy lot redeemer-like; thy heav'n-led hand
  Could wrest the growing shame
  Of thy young country's name
And set bright freedom's halo on thy land!

THE SACRED PROMISE

WHEN the heart shall look beyond its present
  sorrow,
      Then Faith, so blest,
Shall say, "Weep not, all shall be peace to-
  morrow
      For thy beloved; at rest.
      Behold the promise of the Lord,
      The sacred promise of His word:
When thy loved on earth shall turn and leave
  thee,

The Sacred Promise

Then my radiant angels shall receive thee,
In their arms shall angels onward bear thee,
That no evil ever may come near thee!"

Then lift thine eyes, behold a king immortal,
      Whose name is Love;
A light to lead thee thro' the shaded portal
      To His fair throne above.
      Thine is no victory, O grave,
A king hath given his Son to save!
When thy loved on earth shall turn and leave
    thee
Then my radiant angels shall receive thee,
In their arms shall angels onward bear thee,
That no evil ever may come near thee!

A POET'S SACRIFICE

Young Emma was a cultured maid of aspiration
    high;
'Tis said the stars smiled at her birth and
    twinkled in the sky.
The fairies to her christening came, a brilliant,
    glitt'ring throng;
And no one missed (among that crowd) the
    little sprite called Song!

A Poet's Sacrifice

In after years fair Emma's heart held one absorb-
 ing thought
As, to accomplish her great "aim," both day
 and night she wrought.
"Oh, I must touch some glowing theme (this
 was her rev'rie fond);
The slumb'ring ages shall awake beneath my
 magic wand!"

Thus many ballads she composed, and endless
 dramas, too;
While sonnets by the score she wrote; young
 Emma grew so blue!
Ethereal-hued her senses, too, for at the feast's
 fair shrine
Young Emma sat and pondered thus amid the
 courses nine:

"I'll not partake, poor Byron said, it moved
 him to disgust,
To see angelic creatures eat; how sad to think
 we must!
I would that I were far away from all this vulgar
 din;
I really think to-morrow morn an epic I'll
 begin."

A Poet's Sacrifice

As thus she mused her roving eye fell on the
    table good;
"Did Byron really think," she said, "that we
    should have no food?
'Tis plain he overstretched the point, I cannot
    hungry stay";
Fair Emma then began to eat; ye muses, steal
    away;

Henceforth by lone Castilian spring your weary
    vigil keep,
And you, ye shades of vanished song, in saddest
    exile weep.
Alas! that night the parents fond, the friends
    stood 'round a bed
Of one in throes of agony, of one who over-
    fed.

Not "flow of soul" nor "reason's feast" had
    e'er so wrought her brain,
It seemed the outraged muses laughed and
    mocked her in her pain,
With impish glee they filled the room, the
    while her heart did quake,
Quoth one, "I am that 'rosy dawn' whose
    name you often take."

A Poet's Sacrifice

And yet another cried, " Behold ! for oft you've
    called on me
Before you now, in deep disgust, the shade of
    Sappho see !"
At last young Emma strove no more, she called
    her parents dear,
And said, " Now mark, in sympathy, and my
    last wishes hear ;

" I ask that you shall burn my odes, my ballads,
    sonnets, too,
And feed my drama to the goat, and now, ' kind
    friends,' adieu !"
And thus the future's priestess passed, poor
    maid, so erudite,
Some other hand must, later on, the nation's
    epic write.

A ROW ON THE AVON

In the pure light that falls half-way
Between the dusk and light of day,
I walked once more thro' all the place,
The Master's light shall ever grace :
A softened glamor on it lay—
The bower of young Anne Hathaway.

A Row on the Avon

I saw the shadows deeper grow,
And turned away, tho' loth to go ;
For there in that old garden grew
All the flowers Shakespeare knew,
Thyme and Rosemary and Rue !

Yet out thro' clover-scented air,
In thick'ning twilight passed I where
The fair-famed Avon stilly flowed—
Where oft, full oft, the lovers rowed,
As to and fro I saw there float,
I freed a restless little boat :
How long I rowed I may not know,
So sweet-deceptive is the glow,
Of their late English twilight !   Still,
Wan light to moonlight merged, until
The two were one.   Soft sounds I heard
From where the oar had slightly stirred
The water ; later 'twas I caught
A sound of rustling wings, I thought !
But yet, as all seemed calmly clear,
I banished far the idle fear,
And on the still oars rested.   Then
The sounds unknown awoke again—
And straining all the shadow through
I saw two swans of snowy hue
Upon the waters grandly float,
Following close the little boat !

www.ingramcontent.com/pod-product-compliance
Lightning Source LLC
Chambersburg PA
CBHW032359020726
47499CB00008B/2815